CUBA

by Kate Conley

Published by The Child's World®
1980 Lookout Drive • Mankato, MN 56003-1705
800-599-READ • www.childsworld.com

Acknowledgments
The Child's World®: Mary Berendes, Publishing Director
Red Line Editorial: Editorial direction and production
The Design Lab: Design

Design elements: Shutterstock Images; Vladimir Wrangel/
Shutterstock Images
Photographs ©: Shutterstock Images, cover (left bottom),
cover (left top), cover (right), 1 (top), 1 (bottom right) 16
(right), 6–7, 8, 9, 12, 14–15, 19, 20–21, 23, 24, 25,
30; Vladimir Wrangel/Shutterstock Images, cover
(left middle), 1 (bottom left), 16 (left); iStock Editorial/
Thinkstock, 5; Elliotte Rusty Harold/Shutterstock Images, 11;
Ragne Kabanova/Shutterstock Images, 26–27;
Jorge Rey/Getty Images News/Thinkstock, 28

ISBN 9781634070416
LCCN 2014959742

Printed in the United States of America
PA02344

ABOUT THE AUTHOR

Kate Conley is the author and editor of many children's books. She lives in Minnetonka, Minnesota, with her husband and two children. Conley spends many snowy winter days wishing she were in Cuba!

TABLE OF CONTENTS

CHAPTER 1
WELCOME TO CUBA! 5

CHAPTER 2
THE LAND 8

CHAPTER 3
GOVERNMENT AND CITIES 13

CHAPTER 4
PEOPLE AND CULTURES 19

CHAPTER 5
DAILY LIFE 24

FAST FACTS, 30

GLOSSARY, 31

TO LEARN MORE, 32

INDEX, 32

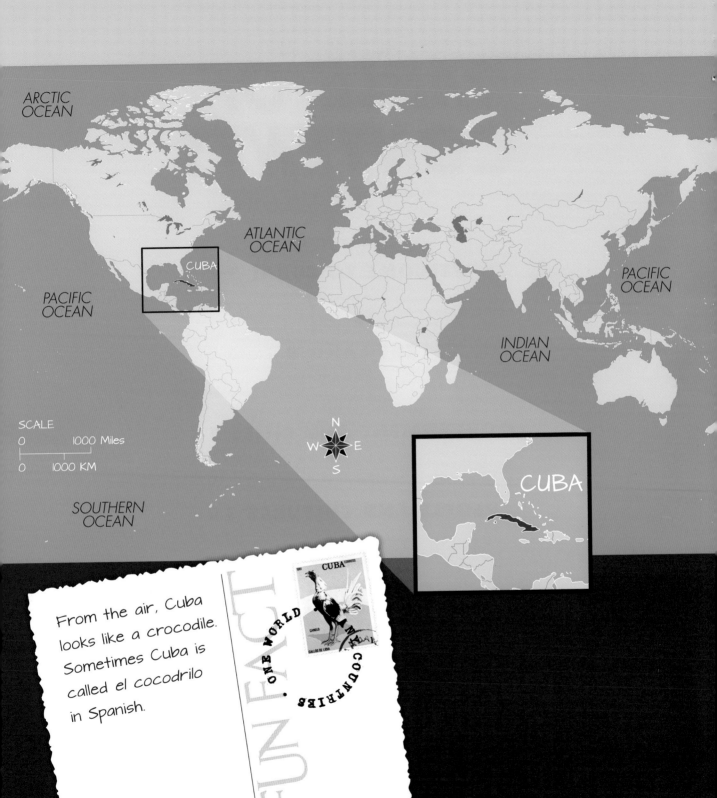

ARCTIC
OCEAN

ATLANTIC
OCEAN

CUBA

PACIFIC
OCEAN

PACIFIC
OCEAN

INDIAN
OCEAN

SCALE
0   1000 Miles

0   1000 KM

SOUTHERN
OCEAN

N
W • E
S

CUBA

From the air, Cuba
looks like a crocodile.
Sometimes Cuba is
called el cocodrilo
in Spanish.

FUN FACT • ONE WORLD IN MANY COUNTRIES

CUBA
CORREOS
CANELO
GALLOS DE LIDIA

CHAPTER 1

WELCOME TO CUBA!

It is a hot evening in late July. Children in Santiago de Cuba line the streets. They dance to music that is growing louder. A brightly colored float makes its way down the street.

The children cheer as the parade finally reaches them. Families worked for months to build the floats in the parade. The first float looks like a giant merry-go-round. On the next float, a ship moves in the wind.

Cubans cheer as each parade float makes its way through the streets of Santiago de Cuba.

Musicians perform in the parade. They play traditional conga music using drums and trumpets. Children in colorful costumes dance to the music. The children smile joyfully.

This parade is especially for children. It is part of a larger holiday for the city's **patron saint**, Santiago. This holiday is celebrated with the National Day of Rebellion. This day honors Fidel Castro. He served as Cuba's leader for almost 50 years from 1959 to 2008.

Many changes took place in Cuba during Castro's time as leader. Nearly all Cubans attended school and learned to read. New hospitals were built and health care

improved. Cuban farmers grew more crops.

Despite these improvements, Cuba still faces many problems. People often do not have enough food or money. People go to jail if they speak out against the government. Many Cubans also miss family members who **emigrated** to the United States.

In 2014, leaders from Cuba and the United States began working together for the first time in more than 50 years. Cubans are hopeful that the changes they make will improve their lives and their country.

Many Cubans live in crowded, run-down apartments.

CHAPTER 2

THE LAND

Cuba's valleys are filled with beautiful trees and plants.

Cuba is the largest island in the Caribbean Sea. It is long and narrow. Cuba is close to several other islands. It is within 55 miles (89 km) of Haiti, Jamaica, and the Bahamas. Cuba is also 90 miles (145 km) south of Key West, Florida.

Mountains cover almost 25 percent of Cuba's land. Trees and tropical plants grow on the mountains. Many years ago,

landowners cleared some of these trees to build farms. These farms continue to grow crops, such as coffee and cocoa.

Plains stretch across most of Cuba. The plains have rich soil that is good for growing crops. Most of Cuba's farms are located on the plains. Farmers there grow sugarcane and tobacco.

The plains lead to the island's shore. The southern coast has many marshes and swamps. Small islands form when coral reefs poke above the ocean's surface.

Cuba has about 3,570 miles (5,745 km) of coastline.

Other parts of Cuba's coast have beaches. Some have rocky shores, but others have soft sand and clear water. They are popular places for sunbathing, fishing, and swimming.

Cuba's shoreline also has many harbors. Harbors are protected areas. Wind and waves are much calmer in the harbors than in the open sea. Ships dock in Cuba's harbors when they bring goods to and from the island.

Ships leaving Cuba are often loaded with nickel, a type of metal. Cuba has more than 30 percent of the world's

nickel supply. It is used to make jewelry, coins, batteries, and electronics. China and European countries buy most of Cuba's nickel.

The weather in Cuba is warm. The average temperature is between 70 and 80 degrees Fahrenheit (21 and 27°C). Strong storms called hurricanes are a danger from June to November. Hurricanes bring heavy rain and strong winds to Cuba. They can ruin homes and flood fields.

Cuba is home to the world's smallest hummingbird. It is called the zunzuncito.

FUN FACT · ONE WORLD · MANY COUNTRIES

CHAPTER 3

GOVERNMENT AND CITIES

Cuba's largest city is Havana. It is also the capital. Havana is located on the northwest coast of the island. One of Havana's best-known areas is the *Malecón*. It is a **seawall** that stretches along Havana's coast. Cubans go to the *Malecón* to relax. On hot days, children jump off the wall into the cool sea below. Adults walk along the wall or sit on its edge and talk.

Havana is also known for its historic buildings. Many are in an area called Old Havana. Spanish settlers built the churches, forts, plazas, and homes there 300 years ago.

Santiago de Cuba is a city on the southeast coast. It is Cuba's second-largest city. Spanish settlers founded it in 1514. Slaves from Africa arrived in this city. Today, the city has Cuba's largest population of people with African heritage.

About 2 million people live in Havana.

Camagüey is a city in central Cuba. When it was first built, it was on the coast. It moved to the center of the country later. The city became rich under Spanish settlers, causing pirates to **raid** the city. The settlers wanted to stop the raids so they built a maze of new streets. This confused the pirates and stopped the raids.

Every Cuban city has a leader. The city leaders must follow the laws of the national government in Havana. Fidel Castro became prime minister of Cuba in 1959. He created a Communist government. It gave free education, great health care, and low-cost housing to all Cubans.

Castro also **nationalized** businesses in Cuba. Individuals could no longer own businesses, such as banks, factories, or stores. Instead, the government owns them. Government officials decide which movies play in the theaters and what food is sold in stores.

Cuba's biggest trading partners are China and Venezuela. Cuba buys trains, buses, and cars from China. China buys nickel, sugar, and cigars from Cuba. Cuba's trade with Venezuela is different. Instead of goods, Cuba sends thousands of its

Cuba's government decides how much all workers are paid.

doctors, teachers, and coaches to the other country. Venezuela then sells its oil to Cuba at very low prices.

Trade with other countries is only one part of Cuba's income. More than half of all families living in Cuba receive money from relatives who live somewhere else. In 2012, Cubans received more than $2.6 billion from relatives in the United States. This money is Cuba's largest source of income.

Cuban currency

Cuban flag

GULF OF MEXICO

THE BAHAMAS

Florida

HAVANA

Ciudad de la Habana

Archipiélago de Sabana

La Habana

Pinar del Río

Matanzas

Villa Clara

Cienfuegos

Isla de la Juventud

CUBA

Sancti Spíritus

Ciego de Ávila

Camagüey

Camagüey

Las Tunas

Holguín

Archipiélago de los Jardines de la Reina

Granma

Santiago de Cuba

Guantánamo

CARIBBEAN SEA

Santiago de Cuba

N W E S

CAYMAN ISLANDS

JAMAICA

FUN FACT

Havana is home to a fortress that was built more than 400 years ago. It protected Havana from pirates. It still stands today.

ONE WORLD · MANY COUNTRIES

CUBA

GLOBAL CONNECTIONS

The United States and Cuba have had a difficult past. For many years, the countries got along and worked together. When Castro took over, U.S. leaders disagreed with him. To show their disagreement, the United States started an **embargo** in 1961.

The embargo stopped trade between the countries. Cubans could no longer buy American goods, such as cars and telephones. Americans could no longer buy Cuban goods, such as sugar. It also made traveling between the countries difficult.

The embargo stayed in place for more than 50 years. That all changed on December 17, 2014. On that day, President Barack Obama made an announcement. He said the United States and Cuba would begin working together.

Leaders of the two nations met to talk about many changes. Both countries want traveling between the nations to be easier. They also want businesses to begin trading again. These changes will slowly be put into place.

Obama and Castro are hopeful. They want the changes to improve life for people in both nations. Obama spoke directly to Cuban people when he said, "America extends a hand of friendship."

CHAPTER 4

PEOPLE AND CULTURES

Cuba is known throughout the world as a lively, colorful country. The people who created this culture come from two main groups. Most people are the ancestors of Spanish settlers or African slaves. Spanish settlers brought their language to Cuba. Today, most Cubans speak Spanish.

Many parts of Cuban life can be traced back to Spain and Africa.

Spanish settlers also brought the Catholic religion to Cuba. Africans also brought their own religions. Catholic and African beliefs slowly mixed and created a religion called *Santería*. It is widely practiced in Cuba, along with Catholicism.

When Castro took over, Cubans could not openly celebrate religious holidays, such as Christmas or Easter.

FUN FACT · ONE WORLD MANY COUNTRIES

Christopher Columbus landed in Cuba in 1492. He wrote about it in his journal. He said, "This island is the most beautiful that I have yet seen."

Castro wanted Cubans to celebrate national holidays instead. Cubans celebrate the National Day of Rebellion on July 26. It marks Castro's first attempt to take over Cuba. On this day, Cubans hear speeches, wave flags, and listen to music.

Music is everywhere in Cuba. Children and adults love to move to the beat. Listening to music and dancing is part of daily life in Cuba.

Cuban musicians often play instruments invented in Cuba. The *tres* is a guitar with three strings. The *güiro* is a

Cuban music mixes African rhythms with Spanish melodies.

gourd that musicians play with a stick. The claves are a set of wooden sticks used to keep the beat.

These instruments are used to make *son* music. *Son* began in eastern Cuba in the early 1900s. Its rhythms and melodies have inspired other types of music, including salsa. Cuba is also known for *rumba* music. African workers on the docks in Havana created it. They used boxes and crates as drums. The rhythms grew to be very popular. Today *rumba* can be heard throughout Cuba.

Cuba's government supports music, dance, and other arts. It provides free classes, supplies, and places for artists to show their work. More than 200 *Casas de Cultura* are located in Cuba. These are spaces for people to learn traditional Cuban arts.

Sports are also funded by the Cuban government. Cuba's national sport is baseball. The country's teams are some of the best in the world. Many children like to watch the games. They also like to play pickup games of baseball with their friends.

The government puts on free arts events, such as ballets and plays.

CHAPTER 5

DAILY LIFE

Many of Cuba's large cities are crowded and not in the best condition.

The majority of Cubans live in large cities such as Havana. City life has many challenges. Many apartment buildings are in poor condition. Not everyone who wants an apartment has one. Electricity, water, and phone services can turn off without warning.

Many Cubans choose to spend most of their time outdoors. It is common to see groups of friends standing on street corners talking. Sometimes families go to the beach for the day. Or they may watch baseball games at an outdoor stadium. Listening to live music outside is also a popular activity.

FUN FACT

ONE WORLD • MANY COUNTRIES

Cuba has 60,000 vintage American cars built in the 1940s and 1950s. The cars arrived in Cuba before the trade embargo.

Few Cubans own cars. Buses are the most common way to travel in a city. Riding a bus costs very little, but Cuban buses can be crowded. They often do not have regular schedules. Many Cubans walk or ride bicycles.

In most families, one person holds a legal job provided by the government. Usually it does not provide enough money for the whole family. Many families create a side business to earn extra money. These side businesses are illegal. Families must be very careful not to be caught.

Families often run these businesses from their homes. They might cut hair, sell baked goods, serve meals, or

take in renters. Most people who run side businesses dislike breaking the law. They feel they have no other choice when it comes to providing for their families.

Shopping in Cuba is different than shopping in many parts of the world. The government issues each household a ration book. Shoppers take the book to a government store to buy food and goods. Ration coupons pay for items such as rice, coffee, eggs, meat, milk, and soap.

Many Cubans hold jobs, such as in factories, but they sometimes have secret businesses on the side to make more money.

Cubans use ration books to pay for many food items, including meat.

Cubans often want goods that the ration books do not provide. They rely on relatives living outside the country to help them. Relatives send items that are hard to find in Cuba. These items include flat-screen televisions, blue jeans, toys, tools, car tires, and shampoo.

With the shortage of goods, Cubans have become creative. Nothing is wasted. Empty toilet paper rolls become hair curlers. Old washing machine spinners are turned into fans. Old flannel sheets are remade into diapers. Cars are expertly repaired to last more than 50 years.

This creativity allows Cubans to face the challenges in their country. They are hopeful life will improve as their nation changes. No matter what the future holds, Cubans take pride in the rich island culture they have created.

DAILY LIFE FOR CHILDREN

For children in Cuba, school is an important part of the day. Children must attend school until ninth grade. The government provides them with uniforms, supplies, and meals. Classes are small and teachers are well trained and respected.

In ninth grade, some students choose to continue studying and go to high school. Others may choose to learn a trade and begin to work. Children talented in art, music, dance, or sports may attend schools that specialize in these subjects.

Cuban children also enjoy their free time. They play outside. Swimming and riding bikes are popular pastimes. Children also like to play stickball. It is a game like baseball that is played in the street. Players use broomsticks or mop handles as bats.

FAST FACTS

Population: 11 million

Area: 42,803 square miles (110,860 sq. km)

Capital: Havana

Largest Cities: Havana, Santiago de Cuba, and Camagüey

Form of Government: Communist

Language: Spanish

Trading Partners: European countries, China, and Venezuela

Major Holidays: National Day of Rebellion and Santiago Carnival

National Dish: *Ropa Vieja* (shredded beef with tomatoes, green peppers, onions, and garlic)

Traditional Cuban outfits are bright and colorful.

GLOSSARY

embargo (em-BAR-go) An embargo is a legal stop to trading. The United States placed a trade embargo on Cuba in 1961.

emigrated (EM-uh-grate-id) To have emigrated is to have left one place and moved to another. Many Cubans emigrated to the United States.

nationalized (NASH-uh-nuh-lized) To be nationalized is to be controlled by the national government. Fidel Castro nationalized Cuba's businesses.

patron saint (PAY-truhn SAYNT) A patron saint is a person believed to protect a particular place. Santiago is the patron saint of Santiago de Cuba.

raid (RAYD) A raid is a sudden attack on a place. Pirates began to raid cities in Cuba.

seawall (SEE-wahl) A seawall is a large wall that protects a shore. Havana's seawall is called the *Malecón*.

TO LEARN MORE

BOOKS

Engle, Margarita. *The Poet Slave of Cuba: A Biography of Juan Francisco Manzano*. New York: Henry Holt and Co., 2006.

Simmons, Walter. *Cuba*. Minneapolis: Bellwether Media, 2011.

Wells, Rosemary. *My Havana: Memories of a Cuban Boyhood*. Somerville, MA: Candlewick, 2010.

WEB SITES

Visit our Web site for links about Cuba: **childsworld.com/links**

Note to Parents, Teachers, and Librarians: We routinely verify our Web links to make sure they are safe and active sites. So encourage your readers to check them out!

INDEX

arts, 18, 22, 29

Camagüey, 14, 17

Castro, Fidel, 6, 14–15, 18, 20–21

coasts, 9–10, 13–14

daily life, 21, 24–29

government, 7, 13–15, 18, 22, 26–27, 29

Havana, 10, 13–14, 17, 22, 24

jobs, 26

music, 5–6, 7, 18, 21–22, 25, 29

nickel, 10–11, 16

Santiago de Cuba, 5, 13, 17

settlers, 13–14, 19–20

sports, 7, 22, 29

trade, 15–16